Essential Science

Circuits & Conductors

Peter Riley

FRANKLIN WATTS
LONDON • SYDNEY

First published in 2006 by Franklin Watts
338 Euston Road, London NW1 3BH

Franklin Watts Australia
Hachette Children's Books
Level 17/207 Kent Street, Sydney NSW 2000

Editor: Rachel Tonkin
Designer: Proof Books
Picture researcher: Diana Morris
Illustrations: Ian Thompson

Picture credits:
Rick Doyle/Corbis: 18; Chet Gordon/Image Works/Topfoto: 23c;
Bob Krist/Corbis: 9; Andrew Lambert/Science Photo Library: 25;
Jose Fuste Raga/Corbis: 22; Benjamin Rodell/Corbis: 27;
Shout Pictures: 20; Sean Sprague/Image Works/Topfoto: 24;
Mike Theiss & Jim Reed/Corbis: 16; Anthony Vizard/Eye
Ubiquitous/Corbis: 26.

All other images: Andy Crawford

With thanks to our model: Gloria Maddy

A CIP catalogue record for this book
is available from the British Library

ISBN-10: 0 7496 6442 8
ISBN-13: 978 0 7496 6442 8

Dewey Classification: 621.319'2

Printed in China

CONTENTS

CIRCUITS AND CONDUCTORS

We use electricity for many things. Think of the last time you pressed a switch. Was it to turn out a light, put on your computer or change the channels on a television set? If we want electricity to work for us we have to let it flow as a current. Materials which allow electricity to flow through them are called conductors.

battery

wires

switch

lamp

When you make a circuit you must make sure that all the components are connected together by the wires.

A simple circuit

Electricity flows in a loop called a circuit. The items that are linked together to make a circuit are called components. There is no beginning or end to a circuit but if there is a gap between any component, the electricity stops flowing and the circuit does not work. A simple circuit can be made with a battery, a switch, a lamp and three wires, as in the picture.

A battery contains a store of electrical energy. When the battery is connected into a circuit it pushes a current of electricity around the circuit.

The wires are made of metal coated in plastic. Metals allow electricity to pass through them. They are conductors.

metal parts

gap

A switch has two metal parts with a gap between them which can be opened or closed. When the gap is closed, electricity flows through the circuit. When the gap is opened, electricity cannot flow.

filament

A lamp has a metal wire called a filament in it that can conduct electricity. When the electric current flows through the filament, the filament glows and the lamp shines.

Mains circuits

The circuits around you in the walls and ceilings of rooms leading to lights and plug sockets are called mains circuits. The electricity that flows through them comes from a power station. In a power station, electrical generators produce huge amounts of electrical energy. They make larger, more powerful currents than batteries. You must never perform experiments using mains electricity. It is dangerous.

power station

home

factory

school

The electricity from a power station travels on overhead cables and underground cables to the mains circuits in homes, schools and factories.

Use the data

When scientists do experiments, they make observations and record them. This information is called data. It may be in a table, bar chart or line graph. Look around your home and make a list of all the different electrical devices in each room and record it in a bar chart. How does your data compare?

Answers to questions in this book are on page 31.

BATTERIES AND CELLS

A battery is a portable source of electricity. You can put it in a torch or an electric toothbrush and carry it around with you. Most of the electrical components we call batteries are cylinder shaped. In science these are called cells.

A cell

This diagram shows the inside of a cell.

POSITIVE TERMINAL
This metal cap is called the positive terminal. There may be a plus (+) sign close to it on the case.

CHEMICAL PASTE
This is a paste which contains chemicals that make electricity.

CARBON ROD
This carbon rod helps in the electricity-making process.

NEGATIVE TERMINAL
This end of the cell is called the negative terminal. There may be a negative (-) sign close to it on the case.

A cell provides electricity to make this calculator work.

Connecting up wires

When a cell is connected into a circuit, one end of a wire must touch the positive terminal and one end of another wire must touch the negative terminal. The current travels round the circuit from the negative terminal to the positive terminal.

Batteries

Two or more cells can be placed in a circuit to increase the push of the current. The cells must be placed with the positive terminal of one cell next to the negative terminal of the next cell. A row of two or more cells in line forms a battery. Some large batteries are box shaped. They contain cells joined together.

Why cells run down

Chemicals in the paste inside a cell take part in an irreversible change as they generate electrical energy. This means they are eventually used up and that is why cells and batteries run down.

Here are five cells of different sizes. Inside the blue container is a battery of two cells.

The power of a cell

The power of a cell to send electricity round a circuit is measured in volts. The symbol for this is V and the power in volts is shown on the side. For example, a cell that has a power of one and a half volts will have 1.5 V written on its side.

Connecting up cells

In which circuit would the bulb light up if you press the switch?

A   B   C   D

SYMBOLS

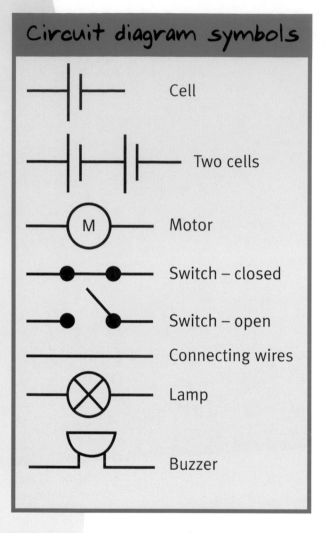

Circuit diagram symbols

Cell	
Two cells	
Motor (M)	
Switch – closed	
Switch – open	
Connecting wires	
Lamp	
Buzzer	

Scientists use symbols to draw pictures of circuits. These can be drawn quickly and are understood by other scientists.

Recording a circuit diagram

When scientists carry out an experiment they also write up a report of what they have done. In the report they may include diagrams. When a circuit diagram is drawn, scientists do not draw each component and the wires bending around between them. They use symbols, as shown. They also draw the wires as straight lines connecting the components together. Some of the symbols for the components you use in making your circuits are shown here.

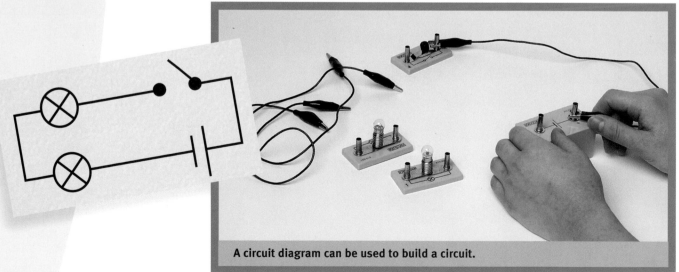

A circuit diagram can be used to build a circuit.

When cells make batteries

There are two vertical lines on the symbol for a cell. The long line stands for the positive terminal and the short line stands for the negative terminal. When two or more cells are connected into a circuit, they make a battery. This is shown with the short line from one cell connected to the long line of the next cell.

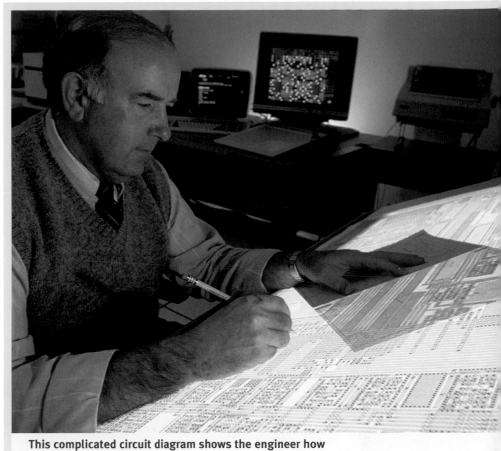

This complicated circuit diagram shows the engineer how the circuit is connected.

Using circuit diagrams

Electrical devices, such as washing machines and televisions, have very complicated circuits to make them work. This means that the circuit diagrams are very complicated, too, but they can be understood by electrical engineers who build and repair them.

Understanding symbols

1 What are the components in this circuit?

2 What will happen when the switch is closed?

3 What would happen if one of the cells were removed and the switch closed?

SWITCHES

**A switch controls the flow of electricity in a circuit.
When the switch is on, electricity can flow.
When the switch is off, the electricity cannot flow.**

Contacts

A switch has two pieces of metal in it with a gap between them. The ends of the pieces of metal on either side of the gap are called the contacts.

metal contacts

You can make a simple switch using a piece of wood, two drawing pins and a paper clip. This switch is open.

Closed and open switches

When a switch is on, scientists say that it is closed. The gap in the switch is closed by the metal contacts being brought together so the current of electricity can flow. When a switch is off, scientists say that the switch is open. The metal contacts have been moved apart and a gap has opened up between them.

A switch allows you to control the flow of electricity in a circuit.

Why switches are used

If a circuit did not have a switch, the wires would have to be joined together and pulled apart to control the flow of electricity. This could damage them. It would be too dangerous to pull apart wires and join them in a mains circuit because the electricity is powerful enough to kill you.

Push switch

A push switch is used in a circuit with a door bell. You push against a spring in the switch to close the gap and ring the bell. When you stop pushing the spring opens the gap again and the bell stops ringing.

contacts

On – closed   Off – open

A light switch on a wall is a rocker switch. The switch on the left is closed as the contacts are touching. The switch on the right is open.

Rocker switch

When one part of the rocker switch is pressed, the contacts are locked together and the switch is closed. When the other part of the rocker is pressed, the contacts are locked apart and the switch is open.

Pressure switch

A pressure switch works by having two contacts with a gap between them. If the switch is pressed the contacts come together to close the switch. Many types of burglar alarm have a pressure switch which is placed under the carpet. When a burglar stands on the carpet the pressure of his weight pushing on the contacts brings them together and closes the switch. The circuit is complete so the alarm rings.

Different switches

Look around for different types of switches. Count up the number of push switches, rocker switches and pressure switches you find. Rocker switches have an on and off position; push switches are like door bells. Draw a bar chart to show your results. Which switch was found the most often?

LAMPS IN CIRCUITS

If you look into the bulb of a lamp when it is switched off, you can see a wire inside it. When electricity flows through a circuit, only the wire in the lamp lights up. This is because the wire in the bulb is made from a special type of metal, called tungsten.

The wire in a bulb is coiled so that a long length can fit inside it and provide a large amount of light.

What happens when electricity flows

Metals contain tiny particles called electrons. These are free to move about. When a metal wire is put into a circuit and the circuit is switched on, electricity makes the electrons all move in the same direction, like people going to a football game.

Why a lamp lights up

The electrons use up energy as they move along the wires in a circuit. When they reach the wire in a lamp they have a problem. This wire does not let them pass through it as easily. It resists the movement of the electrons like a narrow corridor holds up a crowd trying to pass through it. We say it has a high resistance. As the electrons push their way through this wire they use up lots of energy. Some of this energy becomes heat and light energy. This makes the wire glow and become hot.

Two lamps in a row

If two lamps are connected into a circuit in a row they are said to be 'in series'. When electricity flows through them, the resistance of the wire in one lamp adds to the resistance of the wire in the second lamp. This makes it even more difficult for the electrons to move along the wire. They move more slowly and push with less energy and, as a result, both lamps glow less brightly.

The lamps are arranged in a row in a series circuit.

The lamps are arranged side by side in a parallel circuit.

Two lamps side by side

If two lamps are connected into a circuit side by side they are said to be 'in parallel'. When electricity flows through them, the resistance of the wire in one lamp does not add to the resistance of the wire in the second lamp. The electrons push through as if there was only one lamp in the circuit and both lamps shine brightly.

Brighter or dimmer

1 Will the lamps be brighter, dimmer or the same as two lamps in series?

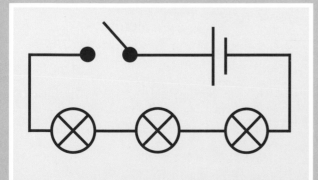

2 Will the lamps be brighter, dimmer or the same as two lamps in parallel?

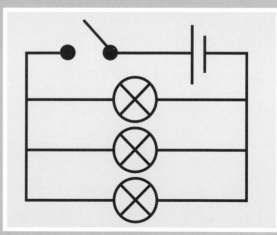

CHANGING CELLS AND LAMPS

A cell supplies a certain amount of electrical power. Lamps work best when they receive a certain amount of electrical power. If they receive too much power they quickly burn out.

Looking for the voltage

The power supplied by a cell is measured in volts and is called the voltage. The voltage of a cell is written on its side as explained on page 7. The power at which a component, such as a lamp, works best is written on its side, too.

DC-6V

The voltages are marked on some of the components of a circuit.

Increasing the power

The power in a circuit can be increased by adding cells in series. For example, putting two 1.5 V cells in a circuit increases the voltage to 1.5 + 1.5 = 3.0 V.

Cells must be added to a circuit by placing the negative terminal of one next to the positive terminal of another.

When a voltage is too low

If a component is supplied with a lower voltage than it needs, it does not work well. For example, a lamp only glows dimly or a motor turns slowly. Increasing the voltage in a circuit can increase the performance of the component, but there is a danger of it burning out.

Adding another cell to the circuit makes the lamp shine more brightly.

When a voltage is too high

If a component is provided with a higher voltage than it needs, the wire inside it becomes very hot and melts. This makes a gap in the circuit and the electricity stops flowing. The heat may also cause other parts of the component, such as a plastic covering, to melt. This can be very dangerous.

Increasing performance

A 4.5 V lamp will glow dimly with a 1.5 V cell in the circuit but will shine very brightly with three 1.5 V cells (that is 4.5 V) in the circuit. If four 1.5 V cells (6.0 V) are in the circuit, the lamp will shine very brightly and then go out when the wire in the bulb melts.

Decreasing performance

A 4.5 V lamp in a circuit with three 1.5 V cells can be made to shine less brightly by removing a cell. It can also be made to shine less brightly by adding a second lamp in series with it. This increases the resistance to the flow of electricity in the circuit (see page 13).

Dim, bright or burn out?

The table shows five circuits with the voltage of the cells and the voltage of a lamp in the circuit. What do you think will happen to each lamp when the circuit is switched on?

Circuit	Voltage of cells	Voltage of lamp
A	3.0	1.5
B	3.0	3.0
C	4.5	6.0
D	1.5	4.5
E	6.0	3.0

CONDUCTORS AND INSULATORS

A conductor is a material which allows electricity to pass through it. An insulator is a material which does not allow electricity to pass through it.

Conductors in a circuit

All the components in a circuit have metal in them which conducts electricity round the circuit.

Testing materials

We can test materials to see if they are conductors or insulators using a simple circuit.

A circuit with a cell, a lamp, a switch and a gap is used to make the test. The switch is opened and the material to be tested is placed across the gap so that it touches the ends of both wires. The switch is then closed and the lamp is observed. If the lamp lights, the material is a conductor. If the lamp does not light the material is an insulator.

buzzer

lamp

motor

All these components contain metal conductors through which electricity can pass.

Air does not usually conduct electricity. However, a storm cloud generates so much electricity that the air around it changes into a conductor and a current passes through it as lightning.

Conductors

When steel, copper, aluminium and iron are put across the gap, the lamp glows. This shows that they are conductors. If the column of graphite from inside a pencil is put across the gap the lamp glows, too. Graphite is not a metal but it does conduct electricity.

Insulators

When wood, plastic or pottery is put across the gap, the components do not work. This shows that these materials are insulators. They are also not metals.

Air acts as an insulator

If there is a gap in a circuit, air fills it. Air is usually an insulator. If you fail to connect the wires in a circuit securely to a component they may fall away and a gap may develop which stops the flow of electricity. This is why it is very important to check all the wire connections if a circuit doesn't work properly.

metal

wood

You can tell if the material in the gap is a conductor or insulator by looking at the lamp when the switch is closed.

What were the materials ?

Five materials were tested in a circuit. A tick means that the lamp lit up; a cross means that it did not light up.

1 Which materials were conductors?

2 Which materials were insulators?

3 Which materials were probably metals?

4 Which materials were not metals?

Material	Lamp
A	✓
B	✗
C	✓
D	✗
E	✗

CHANGING RESISTANCE

Every conductor offers some resistance to the flow of electricity. The resistance acts to stop the current of electricity flowing as strongly.

The resistance in the lighting circuit in a cinema is increased when the lights are dimmed.

Resistance and thickness

The electrons flowing in a circuit move through a conductor like water moving through a pipe. If a pipe is wide, a large volume of water can pass through, but if the pipe is narrow, only a small volume can pass through. In a similar way, a thick conductor can let more electrons pass through it than a thin conductor. This means that a thick conductor offers less resistance to a current of electricity than a thin conductor.

Resistance and length

The resistance of a wire in a circuit also depends on its length. A short wire has a small amount of metal in it to offer resistance. A long wire has more metal to offer resistance. A short, thick wire would make the best conductor.

Changing the number of lamps

The resistance in a circuit can be also be increased by adding more lamps in a series. The metal in the filament of a lamp has a high resistance (see page 12). Each one offers further resistance to the flow of electricity in the circuit.

graphite

The resistance in the circuit of this stereo is reduced when the volume is turned up.

Variable resistors

A device which has a length of conductor that can be varied, like the graphite in the picture, is called a variable resistor. You can change the length of the graphite in the circuit by moving the crocodile clips. If you move the clips further apart, the length of graphite increases and the lamp becomes dimmer. If you move the clips closer together, the length of graphite in the circuit decreases and the lamp shines more brightly. Variable resistors are used in the volume control of a radio or television, and in dimmer switches in homes and cinemas.

How the lamps changed

A variable resistor was placed in a circuit with a lamp. Different lengths of the resistor were put into the circuit and the light shining from the lamp was noted. What do you think was written in the three empty boxes in the table?

Length of wire	Brightness of bulb
10 cm	very bright
20 cm	
30 cm	
40 cm	

PROTECTING CIRCUITS

Too much electricity flowing through a circuit can cause a fire. The circuits in mains electricity are protected from this by fuses.

Fire and circuit damage

When electricity flows through a wire, some heat is produced. Usually it is a small amount and it is not dangerous. If a very large current passes through a wire, a large amount of heat is produced and this can cause materials around the wire to catch fire.

This tumble drier had an electrical fault and caught fire. All the clothes that were inside it caught fire, too.

The current flows through the wire instead of the lamp because the wire has less resistance than the lamp.

The short circuit

If a wire is connected to a lamp, as shown in the diagram, the electricity will flow through it instead of through the lamp. This is because the filament in the lamp has very high resistance and the metal in the wire has low resistance. The current simply takes the path which offers the least resistance. When electricity takes a path in this way it is said to make a short circuit.

Worn cables

A short circuit can happen in worn cables which connect electrical items to the mains electricity. The wires inside the cables are coated in plastic so that the current they carry cannot cross from one wire to the other.

Inside the electrical device are circuits which have a high resistance and they keep the current in the cable wires low. If the cable is worn, holes develop in the insulation around the wires and the metal in the two wires touch. As the cable wires have a lower resistance than the circuits in the device, the current flows from one wire to the other and a short circuit is made.

The wires inside a worn cable can touch each other and cause a short circuit.

The fuse

A fuse is a small cylinder which contains a special piece of wire called a fuse wire. Plugs and electrical devices are fitted with fuses. The fuse wire will melt and break if the current through it gets too large. The broken fuse stops the current like an open switch and stops the device catching fire.

Current size and fuses

The size of a current is measured in units called amps. Electrical devices in the home have fuses to protect them. The fuse will melt if the current exceeds a certain number of amps. Some items take larger fuses.

Arrange the devices in order starting with the one that uses the smallest current.

A oven — 30 amps

B hair drier — 3 amps

C television —13 amps

D iron — 5 amps.

MAINS ELECTRICITY

Mains electricity is used in all kinds of buildings and outside, too, such as in street lights. It is much more powerful than the electricity produced by cells and batteries and can be used for a wide range of tasks.

Lighting

Light bulbs and fluorescent tubes are the two most common forms of lighting. You can find out why a wire in a light bulb gives out light on page 12. A fluorescent tube, such as the lights in schools and offices, has a gas called mercury vapour inside it which is a conductor. This gas gives out energy as rays when it conducts electricity. The rays strike chemicals called phosphors in the tube wall and make them shine. Many street lights have a gas called sodium vapour in them. This is a conductor, too. When electricity passes through it the gas shines with a bright orange-yellow light.

Electricity provides the light for rooms in buildings and for people travelling along the streets.

Heating

Electricity is used to provide heat. There is a coil of wire called a heating element in an electric fire. The coil of wire has a very high resistance. The heating element releases energy as heat when a current passes through it. A hair drier has a heating element and an electric motor in it. The motor spins a fan which blows air over the element to make the air hot so that you can dry your hair.

The electric motor in a hair drier spins a fan which blows air over a heating element to make the air hot.

Movement

An electric motor can make things move. Inside a motor is a coil of wire. When a current of electricity passes into the coil it makes the coil behave like a magnet which makes it spin. The centre of the coil is connected to a shaft which also spins. It is the spinning shaft that provides movement to the wheels of a model car, the turntable in a CD player, the paper moving through a computer printer or to a food mixer.

Comparing power

The power needed to make an electrical device work is measured in watts. The symbol is W.

1 Which device uses the most power?
2 Which device uses the least power?
3 What is the difference in power used between a television and a light bulb?
4 What is the difference in power used between an iron and an electric drill?

Electrical device	Power (W)
Light bulb	60
Television	200
Electric fire	2000
Fridge	150
Iron	700
Electric drill	360

ELECTRICAL SAFETY

The human body is a conductor of electricity. If a large amount of electricity passes into it, the electricity can burn the skin, cause an electric shock and even kill. Great care must be taken with mains electricity

All electrical devices have instruction booklets. These children are following the instructions to use the computers safely.

Plugs

A plug socket should be switched off before the plug is pulled out. The cable should not be tugged to pull the plug out of its socket.

Do not use adaptors to plug a large number of plugs into one socket. This causes a large current to be drawn from the mains. As a large current produces a large amount of heat, the current could cause the plugs and cables to catch fire.

Cables

Cables must not be put under rugs and carpets where they may wear away unseen. They must be kept in view so that any damage can be seen easily. Damaged cables must not be used.

This plug socket is overloaded. A fire may soon start if it was switched on.

Worn cables

A short circuit can happen in worn cables which connect electrical items to the mains electricity. The wires inside the cables are coated in plastic so that the current they carry cannot cross from one wire to the other.

Inside the electrical device are circuits which have a high resistance and they keep the current in the cable wires low. If the cable is worn, holes develop in the insulation around the wires and the metal in the two wires touch. As the cable wires have a lower resistance than the circuits in the device, the current flows from one wire to the other and a short circuit is made.

The wires inside a worn cable can touch each other and cause a short circuit.

The fuse

A fuse is a small cylinder which contains a special piece of wire called a fuse wire. Plugs and electrical devices are fitted with fuses. The fuse wire will melt and break if the current through it gets too large. The broken fuse stops the current like an open switch and stops the device catching fire.

Current size and fuses

The size of a current is measured in units called amps. Electrical devices in the home have fuses to protect them. The fuse will melt if the current exceeds a certain number of amps. Some items take larger fuses.

Arrange the devices in order starting with the one that uses the smallest current.

A oven — 30 amps

B hair drier — 3 amps

C television —13 amps

D iron — 5 amps.

MAINS ELECTRICITY

Mains electricity is used in all kinds of buildings and outside, too, such as in street lights. It is much more powerful than the electricity produced by cells and batteries and can be used for a wide range of tasks.

Lighting

Light bulbs and fluorescent tubes are the two most common forms of lighting. You can find out why a wire in a light bulb gives out light on page 12. A fluorescent tube, such as the lights in schools and offices, has a gas called mercury vapour inside it which is a conductor. This gas gives out energy as rays when it conducts electricity. The rays strike chemicals called phosphors in the tube wall and make them shine. Many street lights have a gas called sodium vapour in them. This is a conductor, too. When electricity passes through it the gas shines with a bright orange-yellow light.

Electricity provides the light for rooms in buildings and for people travelling along the streets.

ELECTRICAL SAFETY

The human body is a conductor of electricity. If a large amount of electricity passes into it, the electricity can burn the skin, cause an electric shock and even kill. Great care must be taken with mains electricity

All electrical devices have instruction booklets. These children are following the instructions to use the computers safely.

Plugs

A plug socket should be switched off before the plug is pulled out. The cable should not be tugged to pull the plug out of its socket.

Do not use adaptors to plug a large number of plugs into one socket. This causes a large current to be drawn from the mains. As a large current produces a large amount of heat, the current could cause the plugs and cables to catch fire.

Cables

Cables must not be put under rugs and carpets where they may wear away unseen. They must be kept in view so that any damage can be seen easily. Damaged cables must not be used.

This plug socket is overloaded. A fire may soon start if it was switched on.

Heating

Electricity is used to provide heat. There is a coil of wire called a heating element in an electric fire. The coil of wire has a very high resistance. The heating element releases energy as heat when a current passes through it. A hair drier has a heating element and an electric motor in it. The motor spins a fan which blows air over the element to make the air hot so that you can dry your hair.

The electric motor in a hair drier spins a fan which blows air over a heating element to make the air hot.

Movement

An electric motor can make things move. Inside a motor is a coil of wire. When a current of electricity passes into the coil it makes the coil behave like a magnet which makes it spin. The centre of the coil is connected to a shaft which also spins. It is the spinning shaft that provides movement to the wheels of a model car, the turntable in a CD player, the paper moving through a computer printer or to a food mixer.

Comparing power

The power needed to make an electrical device work is measured in watts. The symbol is W.

1 Which device uses the most power?
2 Which device uses the least power?
3 What is the difference in power used between a television and a light bulb?
4 What is the difference in power used between an iron and an electric drill?

Electrical device	Power (W)
Light bulb	60
Television	200
Electric fire	2000
Fridge	150
Iron	700
Electric drill	360

Water

Water conducts electricity so you must never handle electrical equipment with wet hands or near water. Do not touch a switch if you have wet hands as water may flow to the contacts and conduct a current to you. The cord of a pull switch in a bathroom is made from insulating material and prevents electricity from the switch reaching your hands. Devices which use mains electricity, such as a radio, must not be taken into the bathroom in case you touch them with wet hands.

Substations have warning signs to keep people away from them.

Power lines

Kites must not be flown near overhead power lines. If a kite becomes stuck on a power line, electricity may pass down the string to the person holding it and give them a large electric shock which could kill them.

Substations

A substation delivers electricity to a neighbourhood and is surrounded by a high fence. Children should not climb over the fence to play on the substation as there is a danger they may receive a fatal electric shock from the equipment.

Electrical safety

Read the scenarios below and decide whether you think the people did the right thing or not. What would you do in that situation?

1 A group of children playing football accidentally kick the ball into a substation. One boy climbs the fence to get the ball back.

2 A woman is changing a light bulb in a lamp. She unplugs the lamp before she removes the bulb and replaces it with a new one.

POWER STATIONS

Mains electricity is generated at a power station. Many power stations use energy from fuel to generate electricity. Some use energy from the wind or flowing water.

Generating electricity

Electricity is produced in a generator. Steam from a boiler pushes on turbine blades and makes them spin. This makes a magnet spin round inside coils of wire. Currents of electricity flow in the coils and are conducted away on cables to towns and cities.

steam · coils of wire · cables · boiler · magnet · turbine chamber · shaft · generator

A power station that burns fossil fuels has three main parts: the boiler, turbine chamber and generator.

Power station fuels

Many power stations burn fossil fuels — coal, gas or oil — to release heat energy and make steam. Burning fossil fuels causes large amounts of harmful gases to be released into the air. This may cause global warming and acid rain which can damage buildings, plants and fish. Some power stations use nuclear fuel. When nuclear fuel is made, it produces harmful rays called radiation. Great care is taken to stop the radiation escaping from the power station. The energy released from fuels is used to heat water and make steam.

A power station burning fossil fuels gives out large clouds of smoke which contains harmful gases.

Water and wind

Some power stations use flowing water to spin the turbine blades. These power stations, called hydroelectric power stations, have a dam built across a river. The water collects behind the dam and is then released through the turbines.

A wind farm is built in a place where strong winds blow for most of the year. Each generator on the farm is mounted on a tall column and has two or more turbine blades attached to it. The wind pushes on the blades and spins them.

Saving energy

Eventually fossil and nuclear fuels will be used up so new ways of generating electricity need to be found. More power stations using renewable energy, such as wind and moving water, may be developed. In the meantime, you can help save fuel by switching off all electrical equipment when it is not in use.

The turbines make a noise and are easily seen in the countryside, but they do not damage the environment by producing harmful gases.

Comparing power stations

The bar chart shows the percentage of electrical power provided by different kinds of power stations in a country.

1 Which kind of power station produced the most electrical power ?

2 Which kind of power station produced the least electrical power?

3 What percentage of electricity was produced from a fuel which has harmful rays?

4 What percentage of power was produced by power stations that affect global warming?

CAN YOU REMEMBER THE ESSENTIALS?

Here you can learn all the essential science facts about circuits and conductors. They are set out in the order you can read about them in the book. Spend a couple of minutes learning each set of facts. If you can learn them all, you know all the essentials about circuits and conductors.

Introduction (pages 4–5)

Electricity flows in a loop called a circuit.
A battery contains a store of electrical energy.
Electricity flows round a circuit through electrical conductors.
The items that are linked together in a circuit are called components.

Symbols (pages 8–9)

Each component in a diagram has a symbol. The symbols of components can be joined together to make a circuit diagram.

Batteries and cells (pages 6–7)

A cell contains chemicals which can generate electricity.
A group of cells make a battery.
A current flows from a cell's negative terminal to the positive terminal.

Switches (pages 10–11)

A switch controls the flow of electricity in a circuit.
A closed switch allows electricity to flow.
An open switch stops electricity flowing.

Lamps in circuits (pages 12–13)

A lamp has a metal filament which has a high resistance. When electricity passes through the filament the filament glows.
Lamps arranged in a row are said to be in series.
Lamps arranged side by side are said to be in parallel.

Protecting circuits (pages 20–21)

Too large a current in a wire can cause a fire. A large current can flow in a short circuit if wiring is damaged. A fuse protects a circuit against a large current.

Changing cells and lamps (pages 14–15)

The power of a cell to push a current is measured in volts. The voltage in a circuit can be increased by adding cells.
Components work best at a certain voltage. If a component receives electricity at too high a voltage it burns out.

DC-6V

Mains electricity (pages 22–23)

Mains electricity can provide light.
Mains electricity can provide heat.
Electric motors change the energy in electricity into movement.

Conductors and insulators (pages 16–17)

A conductor is a material which allows electricity to pass through it. An insulator is a material which does not allow electricity to pass through it. Metals and graphite are conductors. Wood, plastic and pottery are insulators.

Electrical safety (pages 24–25)

Mains electricity can kill. Never touch electrical equipment or switches with wet hands. Do not overload plug sockets. Keep away from overhead power lines and substations.

Changing resistance (pages 18–19)

If the resistance is high, a small current can flow. If the resistance is low a large current can flow. The resistance of a wire can be varied by altering its length or thickness.

Power stations (pages 26–27)

Electricity is produced in a generator in a power station.
Many power stations use fuels.
Some power stations use flowing water.
Wind is used to produce electricity at a wind farm.

GLOSSARY

Amp a unit used to measure electric currents.

Battery a group of cells joined together.

Cable a large thick wire which conducts electricity overhead. A group of thick wires coated in insulation material which conducts electricity underground. A small number of thin wires coated in plastic which are used to connect electrical devices such as computers and printers to the mains and to each other.

Cell a metal cylinder containing chemicals that can make electricity flow in a circuit when the switch in the circuit is closed.

Circuit a loop made by connecting electrical components together so that a current of electricity can pass through them.

Conductor a material that allows an electric current to pass through it.

Contact a piece of metal in a switch which is made to touch a second contact so that electricity can flow in a circuit.

Current the flow of electricity in a circuit.

Electrons tiny particles inside conductors which move in one direction when a circuit is switched on and make the current of electricity.

Energy something which allows an object or a living thing to take part in an activity. It may be moving or giving out light.

Filament a thin wire with many coils used in a lamp to provide light when electricity flows through it.

Fuel a material which releases energy that can be used to make machines, such as electrical generators, work.

Fuse a device with a metal wire in it which melts and breaks if a large current passes through it.

Generator a machine which produces a current of electricity.

Graphite a material made from a black substance called carbon.

In parallel the arrangement of components that are wired up side by side in a circuit.

In series the arrangement of components that are wired up in a row in a circuit.

Insulator a material that does not allow a current of electricity to pass through it.

Irreversible change a change that takes place when one material (or more) changes and cannot be turned back again to the original material.

Metal a substance with a shiny surface which conducts electricity.

Phosphors materials which give out light when struck by rays made inside a fluorescent lamp.

Resistance a property of a conductor to slow down the flow of electricity through it.

Terminal a point on a cell or battery where a wire is connected to form a circuit.

Variable resistor a device which can control the amount of electricity flowing through a circuit by altering its resistance.

Voltage the power of a cell, battery or generator to produce electricity. Voltage is measured in volts (V).

Watts a unit used to measure power (W).

ANSWERS

Batteries and cells (pages 6–7)

B and D

Symbols (pages 8–9)

1 3 cells, a switch and a buzzer.
2 The buzzer will make a loud noise.
3 The buzzer will make a quieter noise.

Switches (pages 10–11)

Rocker switch.

Lamps in circuits (pages 12–13)

1 Dimmer.
2 The same.

Changing cells and lamps (pages 14–15)

A Shine very brightly then burn out.
B Shine very brightly.
C Shine brightly.
D Shine dimly.
E Shine very brightly then burn out.

Conductors and insulators (pages 16–17)

1 A and C.
2 B, D and E.
3 A and C.
4 B, D and E.

Changing resistance (pages 18–19)

20cm bright.
30 cm dim.
40 cm very dim.

Protecting circuits (pages 20–21)

B, D, C, A.

Mains electricity (pages 22–23)

1 Electric fire.
2 Light bulb.
3 140 W.
4 340 W.

Electrical safety (pages 24–25)

1 Wrong – the boy should have left the ball where it was as it is dangerous to go near substations.
2 Right – the woman stays safe by turning off the flow of electricity to the lamp before changing the bulb.

Power stations (pages 26–27)

1 Coal-fired power station.
2 Oil-fired power station.
3 15%.
4 65%.

INDEX